"Trails in the Water on the Shores of the Sun"

By Matt Burrus

To: Amy Ouimet

With this book I tried to steer away from the angst and I have done... fairly well. The jumbled ideas and phrases of this book make me happy, and I hope it makes the reader smile.

- Matt

A Collection of 73 Poems written by Matt Burrus from 2016 to 2018.

Cover art by Regen Waldman 2018, whose huge creative capacity and ruthless role as late-night editor has helped make this book possible.

The characters are nicknamed 'Our Subjects' and their illustrations are by Regen Waldman and are his response to the poems and prose. They share the writing with you and are, in a way, part of the journey.

Text Copyright ISBN 9781725942516

(This cape cannot blow in the wind
Without flipping over my face)

Water, our shared obsession. The Sun, our energy. These two essentials come together to create everything we know and are, including this book. Inspired by water and the sun, this book is dedicated to the impact of these things on my life.

While writing this book I've ended my self-imposed celibacy, met a woman, roamed the world, screamed up cliffs and over mountains, met several good cats, flown into thunderstorms, reacquainted myself with success and learned to be frank.

Trying to pin down a theme in my writing, I realized I was becoming obsessed with two of the factors most present in my daily life. Creating this book has been like focusing a river on a single point and I am so happy to be able to share it with you.

I wrote this book for myself, this book wrote itself for you. Please re-read often and write in the margins.

-Matt

I am the night
You are the day
In the twilight and dawn
We play

Our stories, connected
Shared with colour and shaded tones
As deep as our souls are rooted in our bones

Sometimes we switch sides
You the night
I the day
And still in the dawn and twilight
We play

Far above the stars sing in time with our dance
For the day cannot deny the night
Nor the night shun the day
In perfect harmony they stay

Equal and unbound
Unity through individuality
Hope for times endless possibility

Encouraged and anchored
The realm of feelings and thoughts
The past brought up
The clarity
A revision of techniques
Of tactics

An anger validated
A seclusion accepted
Farms opening their fields for the sun
The land soaking up the spring runoff

Separate trails to the same place
A fast realization of time and space
This section of selection
A conversation woven not between the lines
But in the open, frankly

Great is the scope
Another time
So grateful to be alive
Thank you

Our Subjects

Believing that life is constant
And will remain after we go is
Self-effacing in a irresponsible way
It doesn't matter, your life or your actions
Everything matters
Everything IS everything and we are all
Continually cascading into/through/out of others

Sweeps
Like a broom pushing leaves
From my mind
Always returning for that second swipe
To retrieve what was missed
Sometimes she still scythes through my mind
An apparition
Wholesome this continued pain
The scab strengthens
Puts you in another light
2 years without
Devout, while not puritanical
I could be commended
For my dedication
The end may be in sight
The rebirth of a part, my core
Vitality
Larch trees lying about their deaths to the eyes of those unlearned
I am still alive
I am still breathing in my own way
I can become the skyline
Until the broom comes again to sweep lightly
Away my fallen needles

(Written while building my van - 2017)

Parts of a whole
Eaten in one bite

I cannot become a meal
Stretching the stomach to
Sustain a hunger

For to be completely satisfied
Is to be asleep
Numb to the rigors of others below
The struggle forgotten

Blissfully yearning
    (while in this)
Troubled patch
Discontentment personified
Sections peeled away
Actions examined sober
All given 'the benefit of the doubt'

Poorly drafted,
These life plans
Never have been
Measured and Sectioned
But rather feeling
And happenstance
Carry me

Life cannot be more fragile
Than it seems now
Sitting here I am almost as close to
The other side
As the creature dying in front of me

The light turned off in its eyes
Reflection of intent
Bursting the bubble of
Happy ignorance

It snuffs out
Another light
Forever dark

A few seconds
No different
To anyone else
Until those seconds
Are their last

Recovered from the icy
Chill of the metal box
My mind sheltered within
I cannot see anything
Other than the glass floor
That separates us from
Oblivion

Trails in the water on the shores of the sun
The fish watches the dark clouds
Form without fail
Without opposition
As they so often have
Knowing that it might not effect his world
If he dives deeply
To create a space far away

Yet he cannot tear his eyes away from the coming storm

Blended, the nerves in my shoulders
Glass fragile in this frigid
Space
My mind dwells inside
A decision to reject social blathering
Closed eyes only make the black circles seem bigger
I   can   only   drink   this   water
Eat this place
Word count exceeded after 1

Drifting across a surface
Of proper tones,
Gold and topaz shine below.
And above, beyond the dyslexic dreams
(Where every escape rocket is flown in the wrong direction)
Floats the mercy of a storm
"O construct of my subconscious,
Hear me not!"

For I will not survive without
The nothing that I crave
Connection will be my sword
Pointed inward, let it run me through
As I bleed my protective juices from both sides
Agonizing about how I will not be able to soak it all back up
Let me stagger
Until it is absolutely gone

Free from traffic
My cloud of clarity can travel
Building nothing, for that is its prey
The illusion of expectations
Like blue skies to the deep-sea fish
Cast away and into this way of being
The rejection of 'Potential energy' doing nothing
And the embodiment of the Kinetic

Plastic sunglasses
Used with white paper for a hat

Can the deep grass feel the same
Two years ago
In another lifetime it seems
That the pleasures of sounds
And experience
Can taste different
Exist different
Become another way of living

A hunger a want //

Carved through a endless stream of bubbles
The result
Of letting everything go
The beat of feet on pavement
The stride beneath my waist
Non-conforming to my top-half
In a kind of rebellious manner

Breathing increases and sweat pours down my face
Only a wind
To dry the skin
-To destroy -To protect\

"What a bad shape you are in
      What a good time to sit alone and listen to another
                                similar song"

Keeping a screen close by at all times
I cannot wait without peering into the depths
Cannot pass the time
Glazing out and misunderstanding the grandeur
Of everything

A hunger a want
I can feel it sometimes
The need to let go
To let my conscious mind release the track
It was on

        A break in a language built to distract

"Awake"
Another life ahead
With its intricacies
And its woes

It cannot be escaped
You must go on
Beneath the passion
Repetition clouds the inner landscape
Like an autumn rain

An M followed by an N
The alphabet of existence
Moving through the motions

Samples of snapshots
Bursts of life
And the mundane
Saturating and solidifying

Every affliction suffered
Each life, a new disaster
Depressions within a flat section of ground

The grass is always green
Everywhere the screaming
Of joy and pain
The human existence
Yours to revel in

Muscles crack and sinews strain

The grinding between the present and the past
The future is only a myth
But my god the past can follow us
Like a scared rabbit
Or a crazed fanatic

The ever- present actions of past humans
Our legacy of lunacy
And love
A part of our delirious existence

The rules that you must play by
The features to upgrade
The packages and platinum prices
Our time converted into coin

Below my serenade
Another mother gives birth to the future
Below my suspicious opinions
Another baby crawls with purpose

Muscles shaping into thoughts
Actions
Legends

Attached to empty distance
Watching the fields sprint by
Or slowly slide beneath my feet

Naked or clothed
A clothesline moves in a wind
That has been blowing over old snow
Ice long forgotten

The green grass here to stay but a moment
A Polaroid shaken
And added to the pile

The swing and pluck
Of your voice
Feels good along my spine
The way a comb
Feels through dry,
long hair
finally unknotted

Quality left behind
A season of dry erase-board-sounds
The desert sands grinding
Beneath the rubber
Of worn shoes

A certain freedom
Walking from dirt to gravel
From gravel to snow
And from snow to rock

Upward
Tired sensations catapult
The weary mind
Through the day

Dusk and dawn
The difference between places
Astounding
The environment
And its affects
Talking to oneself
While patiently
Waiting for the rain to pass

The butterflies
With their sail-like wings
And unparalleled competence
Thrum past my head
After navigating branches
Without any sign of effort
Gliding with a purpose
Known only to them

                Boundless blue
                Two birds soaring together
                Into the thermals
                Circling they pass close to
                One another
                Then they are gone from view
                Into the boundless blue

A lifetime of accomplishment
Watching the leaves
Slowly weave
Their wordless dance
In the wind

To watch the sun set
The shadow provided by the peaks
Around me
Slowly moves higher
Until twilight
Reigns

(Nuevo Leon, Mexico 2017)

There is a sphere
A globe
Of friction
Between people
And to deny it exists
Gives it power
To embrace it
And become a vast ocean
Accepting the garbage and dangerous
Currents within
Can be the best
Uncomfortable
Solution

Make it
You cannot
Without sections taken
away
Seeds for something
else
But you must replace
them
With stronger
Feelings
Love and pain
Hate
To feel nothing
To feel everything
Don't identify

I cannot wait for the
Jolt
Epiphany is a slow thing
It is broken down into
Sections
The past may keep to itself
And become a wild
Unkempt thing
Much like the future
However lacking in electricity
My actions cannot stop
From moving me forward

Communicate with the sturgeon
    Breathe slow
        With black eyes
            Rolling your spine
                Slightly to stay moving

    A hundred years can be an eternity
    Under the water
    Below the surface
    Time can be a myth
    Told by other beings

Whiskers and scars
    Can tell stories
        Beyond those around you
            The leading edge of your fins

    Whitened by the flow of the currents

(Written in the Bio dome in Montreal 2017)

Cast me down
The over abundance of health
happiness
growth
Feels like a roller coaster ride
This tide
Comes up and down
The beach in my mind
Sometimes dark with shadow
The swift search for friends near
Becomes frantic
As life hides for a moment
Ere the times of men come to a close
I want to have you
By my side

The moonrise at night
Sometimes comes after
We have gone to sleep

And our eyes are shut
Drama unfolding unnoticed as time
Sneaks
By
    A stranger

In the night walking past

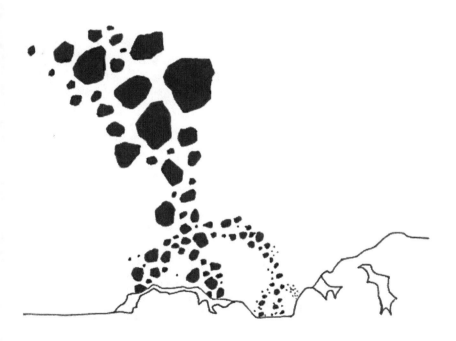

season

Red diamonds
These stones
In peoples hearts
Grind together
To start
Infinite fires
In realms
To obscure to recognize

As the frozen ones seek
To remain
A new order arises
Of flame
And the heat of the heart

Wherever they go
Icebergs cannot escape

A momentary glance into myself
Sand dunes piled high
Amidst the onerous sun
The statues of shadow
Created one by one
Each waiting to die
By the reveal of light
And to be born once again
The next day
The next circular night

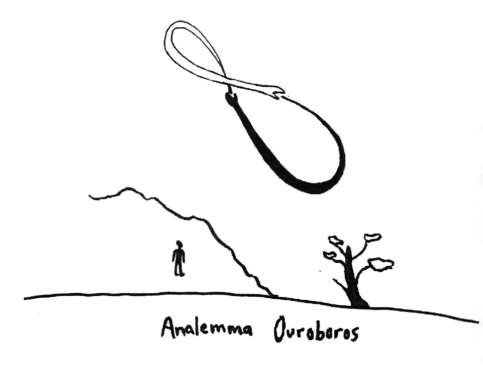

Analemma Ouroboros

Sentimental shadows
A moon encapsulates
The dreams of many
That the small can defy the large

Large winds grow stale
Within the fading sunlight
A darkness not unlike the dusk
Settles across our immediate
Surroundings

A sliver of silver sun
The world feels like it is
Coming under a cosmic
Shadow
That encompasses our souls

Past the flippant conversation
The hiccups within the mind
Grow larger
As the noise subsides

Brushing past my mind
Is the need to hide
And escape this unnatural
Moonless moon
Sunless sky

(Idaho 2017 total solar eclipse)

Slowly creeping, the rain
Soaks every surface
The cement house
Stands up to the barrage
But the cold seeps through the structure

The haze and therefore
A shield from the
Bright shining sun
Lies across the heavens
Without touching my eyes
I can feel its presence
And blue the break
'ore hours of violet white
Unleashed without
The cozy trap of stormy weather
A sailor bound within my vessel
And tempted not
To venture forth

I climb upon this hill of guilt
My conscience, transformed
By the landscape that surrounds me
I sleep the day and the night
While fathoms above are plunged far beneath
The weight of new snow

The autumn stunted
Blown down and bowed before
An ancient power
Limestone shattered and broken
Swept away before the coming of
The cold and the snow

(A winter storm in autumn 2017)

I shall be far away
Holding onto the loose rock
Standing amongst the
Craven moss
Yellow as mustard
Green as algae
Mixed to provide footing
Oh, ere the dawn not seen
But again blossoming
Stout boredom
A rocky shore
To throw myself against
Once more

Mishappenings

Shaken slides fall over
With children still on them
The bolts rusted in the snow
Drip orange down onto the white

Dyslexia spins around my head when I am tired
Pardon the intrusion
My mind suffers from a fog
I must have hit it somewhere

The painful truth of the cold
Is not easy to escape
Blood pooling, cooling

Escape to the tree line
Filthy mothers
Roaring, will come out
Eager to hunt
'The ones responsible'
Or anyone at all

1.) The blind reasoning implied
In every action
Bereft of logic
Somehow positioning your reality
Becoming a deep pool
After many shallow steps
Heavy, barely floating
Too weak to lift
The Capitan of your environment
A prisoner in every interaction
Blasé

2.) Keeping to the light between the shadows
Getting off on the collective mind
Disconnected beyond another door

3.) Faith in your steel will
Crumpled like saran wrap
Resonance amplified under a tin hat
Believing in – creating
As a creature of the night avoids the sun
The moon a mild annoyance

4.) Beyond a selfless connection to each other
Under the beguiling sheet of 'competition'
Down under the sap well of self pity
The core frequency resides
Becoming part of another sound
Broadcast ever so quietly
Across every variation
Of distance

      The winds pour over me
My mind- slight and gaunt
I drift with them
Slandering those stuck below

      Knowing not path
      Nor direction
      Becoming more self-aware

Without words
Inspired action
I cannot believe where my feet
      Have taken me

Like an egg I must be cracked open again
Believe me
I feel numbed with routine
And before my senses return
Know that only you float within
The dark pool of my mind
Floating around, bouncing off the inside of my skull

I feel some orange colour
Some purple
A wave of senses and feeling
Around the corner
Peeking at them
I come closer to living
To being alive

Beauty is an extension
Of being
Of existing complexly
As myself

You cannot believe the feelings you inspire
But I want you to see them
Without showing you

My love
Cannot become lesser
Only more full

Crying
I have so many words for you
Words to spin into carpets
Into lovely paintings
My god
I have not created with my hands
In some time
I need to become again
My open self

While I listen to things grow around me

Over a small-disassembled lamb
A large alligator is standing
Between the ferns
On its back legs
It looks the part
Part villain
Part actor

Stumbling around
I watch the large clouds merge above me
A vicious cycle of
Half circles that seem to
Always be above my head

I cannot collect the light from the darkness
So I will stay here
Until I move along

There are thirty different types
Of hunger
I can remember

But the worst/best
Is the hunger for nothing
While doing something

And the best/worst
Is the hunger for something
While doing nothing

(Glossed over
 the exceptional quality of humans
  generally goes unnoticed)

Currents
Of people
Steeped within styles not their own

Blue and green- like water
The tones and the smells
Waft through the space between us

Brush past them like intrusive cedar branches
The eddies and the swirls
Looking for a purpose
Not given but created within

Circles
Circles
Circles   in the water

> It will happen if you want it to
> Every experience can, and will happen
>
> It cannot be forced
> Your timeline is your own
> Everything happening in a void
>
> It will happen when it happens
> Don't rush for others

(Written for my sister 2017)

To have no reason
But to devote your energy
To become stronger
It is an immense task
The road to improvement
A winding one
With many chances to stop along the way
For when 'goals' are met
The chance to slow presents itself

'All Parts of Time'

I think the greatest expanse is inside ones mind
Another great leap within the gyrating, wholesome
Ubiquitous nature of man
And woman
Belief in another realm of expression

Translation between this reality of limited movement
And another timeless one of life and movement over
and over

Translation;

/// Eden had a son
They named it god
Split it in twain
One to rule the present
One to break it again and again and again

Begot from separation
One began to walk
And each step he took was cut out of the sand
From behind him
Never to be accessible again

Furious, *One* tried to walk backward
Intent upon the force resisting him
As its footprints again disappeared
One said
"By my own hand,
    My past is swept away"

Troubled by this one-way path
One decided to forget about it
And cast itself forward with such speed
Even its mind was left behind

Darkness swallowing noise and sight
Gelatinous night
Beyond the cavernous maws of death
Eden was waiting there
Flaxen hair
Comfortable inside death
As it was her lair

Continuing
One ran 'a single hairs' breath
Faster than its other half

Turning 'round, *One* saw
The gleam in its Brothers' eye as it lit the darkness
And *One* took one real
Step
Back

One connected with its Brother
The present colliding at full speed with the past

In this moment of confusion
Eden observed that the *One* that was *Two*
Became *Three*
And each went their separate ways

Repulsed by a chase through mortality
And a collision with the void
The three would always
Keep their distance
As observed by Eden
And her children ///

Our time is our child
Our lives a product of our creations
Because the fear of 'no return' fuels our focus on the future
Because there cannot only be the past
There must be more corners and crannies
To peer into
Another amiable failing

(All Parts of Time)

Pine needles
Pin pricks of attention
Cedar boughs
the smells
the immersion

Freedom hinges on perception
While I hang it up for a season
It awaits me

Among the Cedar
And the Pine

People

Stella Laguois
Stood apart from the others
Her accent stood out before people noticed her eyes
One blue one white
Blinding colourless pupil
She could see other things with that eye

Poe Pamillar
Watched with trepidation as his car slid off the cliff
In his ear buds
Classical staccato notes kept his ears alive
The plummet was seconds
Stretched into an eternity

Harim Hasrember
Could not stand walking in sandals
His feet felt dirty and coarse
He could not wait to step into the water
Just… where was the water?
All he could see was sand

Chella Strand
Sat at a piano
Without legs
She and the piano
Were two of a kind
And they could talk about restrictions of movement
Their language a combination of clefts, treble and bass

Albert Tranf
Stood at the pinnacle
Before he could reach for more
'What was before is not anymore'
Boomed out across the sky
Through his chest
He left without taking another forward step

He stood.

Not moving with the tides, not singing praises to the ever-brightening light. He was just standing, dreaming of a longing for anything at all.

Not wanting, no, because wanting implied a choice to be had. And he didn't mean 'needing' either, which implied a lack of something.

No, he was just a man, standing where those who looked upward, gazed toward with unwavering passion and hope.

"This place." He thought. "*This place makes my dreams stand still and evaporate into the dusk imposed by my solitude.*"

Suddenly a blinding light blasted the vision from his open eyes, unprotected and unfazed, as the UV rays burned away his retinas.

Still he stood even as his tears evaporated, the light enveloping him.

"*There has to be something more.*" He thought.

"*A place of peace just for me.*"

~~~~~~~~~~~~~~~~

Belonging to the light held no surprises for him. The pain continued, the disconnection maintained, even without a body and becoming the light itself, he was unsatisfied.

""*I cannot shake it/ Beyond the final door is more of the same/ another way to exist unresolved*""

Resuming stillness he poised this question:

""*Energy/ Space/ Nothing changed/ How do you exist satisfied/ Unresolved, my core cannot continue.*""

""*Instruction/ Pain/ THOUGHTS/ No, Not the way.*"" Was the response.

""*Until the question leaves/ leave behind the mind*""

The soft smooth sand
The bubbles scattered across it
Seagulls and sunlight
Mix together among the blue
And lower
The tiny rivulets
Their courses always a little different
Chart backward ways to the ocean
This sweeping curve
A boundary between worlds
Between ways of thinking

Tiktaalik roseae

- Weight-bearing elbows, bending wrist.
- Head capable of independent motion.
- Large ribs to support itself out of water and to support changes to respiration.

It is nothing
Knit together
The frames of life
All so different
Salt fills my nostrils
Where only there was dust before
Another anthem
Thrums through my veins
The absence of anxiety

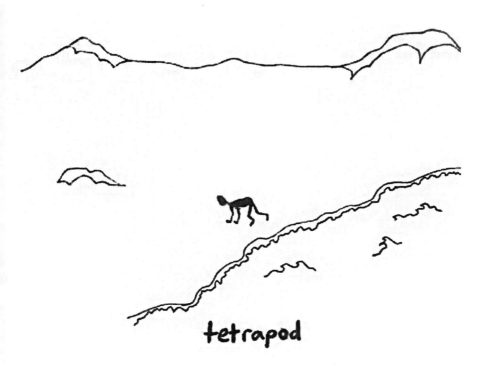

Incapable Carnivores

Cutting under their stare
To wonder
Another person
Added to a list
Of those never to meet again
Careful, the desire is excessive
Belonging to another
Section
Guided by access granted by my
Integration into society
The average so low
The best so much lower
Scoured and pitted
Belching ignorance with every breath
Between bites of 'digestible' news
Rambling about my intelligence
Proving yet- another idiot
Succumbed to gratuitous vanity
Provided within the circles
We build for ourselves

>Harpy-like the spectre of distraction Looms
>Annoying in its hypnotism
>Curious, the prey become ensnared
>Jealous crowds infected
>With the fear of missing
>Nothing but empty air

Wallowing notes
Watery beer
Vapid disconnection from themselves
A section of time never recovered
Believing that choice can be maintained
With an addiction to anything
Other than the lack of everything
Thoughts are discarded as half chewed Morsels
Without scrutiny
Conversations disappear from Consciousness
As if they were never there

The echoes of dissonance
Reverberate through my skull
Sentences cannot be formed
Without a clear effort of will

I have so many People
             Buildings
             Lands
Stuck in my heart

If I am to remember them
I must cut through my insides
Break down my marrow
Just to access them there

If I am born of
Discovery
I must become myself

There are so many People
             Buildings
             Lands
Stuck in my heart

The sun reached out a hand
And brought the cold snow
As fine as sand
Black the sky became
And once again
Belief in daylight waned

Breaking the pull of the
south
The snow turned soft
Branches bloomed white
Another harvest
Ripe

All thoughts of summer faded
The lush forest
Where gaps before
Now filled in
Traverse the garden
Sample what grows there

Write something nice/ can you?

"You have to be able to take it or leave it,
and then you take it"

part of a partnership
instead of a sole survivor
two where there could be one
a simple value
no more than
the most beautiful
woman
no less than
the beautiful liberation
within a connection

"Be frank with me my darling"

~Her hair strummed upon the light
In a statement of grace
The frame, her face
The style, beyond bed sheets
Covers left on the floor

~Heating pads and hot tea
A winter spent with you
Careful in my attachment
But beyond a simple attraction
Love a banished foreign concept until now

~New techno softly spread out across the walls
Like butter over hard bread
Showers and steam baths
Escape the cold
Dive into the snow and shadow

~Her hair summed up the darkness
The clouds of that most recent storm
Swirling around the ceiling
Providing a reason
Simple and serene

I want to strum
To move from one chord to another
Like a slow step.... step
And jump

From a small ledge
A rope or water
Catching my body
And another to catch my soul

To strum and become the music
Through action
Through life
And my fingers
That can become the soul
Of something a little bigger than me or
You

And then we can say that the night was
passed
In a good way
No matter the drinks or the friends
In the end
The music has the sway

Sometimes when I go to sleep
    I get a very powerful feeling that
    I will never wake up again
    Viewing the room
    As a prison
    And my life as something
    That is slowly slipping away from me
    And I can't breathe as I fall asleep
    My stomach knotted

Sometimes my contacts won't focus
    For a few seconds
    And I am forced to remember
    That I am almost blind
    But fooling myself
    Most of the time

Sometimes I feel I have wasted the hours in a day
    That there is no way to get them back
    And when I remember other 'wasted' days
    I feel saddened
    Knowing that these hours not long since passed
    Will not be seen again

Sometimes I suddenly realize
    That the people around me are actually
    My friends
    And it shocks me deeply
    Realizing that I have friends
    And that these are the ones that I have

Sometimes Sometimes Sometimes
    I can't forget
    The words I've said
    But mostly I forget them instantly
    Once they are out of my head

My shoes have been getting wet
Everyday I have to dry them
The way of looking at the ground
Should help me with...
Identifying the most important
Grooves in the concrete
And the little weeds that can grow up through
The major success of the song
Is the bass line
And the singer
And how they can make you notice little things
On the ground
And appreciate them

   Minimalist guitar is my favorite
Making things with my hands
Eating food I have cooked
And sleeping next to you
Calling you on your shit
And listening to you appreciate
Those little cracks
In the concrete

There are phrases
Clipped and chiseled into perfection
The very cream, cropped from atop
The frothing lather
Of lesser works

The sentences of sublime structure
An island in the abyss of language
Scant seconds on the tongue
Ever after on the mind

Flat these trees grow
As flat as needed
For the wind would crush them otherwise
And the moss would consume their
Bodies into the earth

But wiry do they grow
And their bark a raspy scythe
That your hands will not soon forget

Branded as lesser
They are opportunities to learn
To observe
The success of these
Is no small accomplishment

The grass was smooth

As of the till and tide

Low the beach wide

And again the silence

Far and away

*Begone
is my
anger*

*My sheath of
solitude*

*(Building in its complete
Tamed, the spice a smolder
Rage not withstanding)*

*My perch afforded me peace
And vision
To continue*

I am hollow, empty as a wind blown shopping bag
Ejecting air
Permeable and strangely ridged
The grass pokes through the soles of my feet
When I fall asleep I dream in circles
Patterns and shapes I've known too well
To many words left forgotten

Vitality, oh the word leaves me without a breath
Grinding below the weight of my own ego
Hidden between thoughts
Unacknowledged
Now. I. Can. Only. Escape.
This wretched world through the eye of a seagull
The breathing of a single wasp
Tattered moths and crumpled rodents
The ones forgotten

Hollow, my insides are added to the pile
Again I am to damn dramatic

~Ùlger listened to the wind
And tried to taste it
On his tongue

The spies of the kelp
And the herring
Thwarted his efforts
Twisting the wind away

So Ùlger went on
Traversing the rocks
As he had been taught
By his long dead mother
Her fair hair always matted by the spray

He slipped once but soon was out of the sea
And on the land
Picking out which rocks were big enough
To hold his weight

The matters of time and food did little
To distract him from his mission
And the years passed him without notice
For the hunger in his stomach was only
For the wind

It called to him
Just beyond reach
A phantom without form
A specter of hopes and dreams
Just waiting for him beyond the next fjord

You can still watch him search
See his ghost walk the empty beaches
At low tide
And hunt everlasting
For a taste of the wind~

A shrill note
Hung above the stone
Forever
The song played across the clearing
A single sound
Among the graves

Purpose for the day
Lost along the way
My steps brought me to the butchers shop
Large and red
The display case reminded me of
Lovers
Caught in the act of play
Secrets becoming scandals
Victorian values
A common flower
Pressed between the stained pages
Of a porno mag
Stuffed behind a dresser

Feeling lethargic
Bleary eyes
Watch the sun with suspicion
Waiting for the night to come
Rest at last

A blunt curve
Bleeding speed
Crumpling
Into the asphalt and gravel

Smoke clogs the sounds beneath my feet
Dust and grime
Mix in the air
I'm used to it

42 57
Another great
Lovely day
Ticks away

Below the signs
A steady thrum
My nerves at rest

Lovely resources
Spent again and again
The privilege becomes us

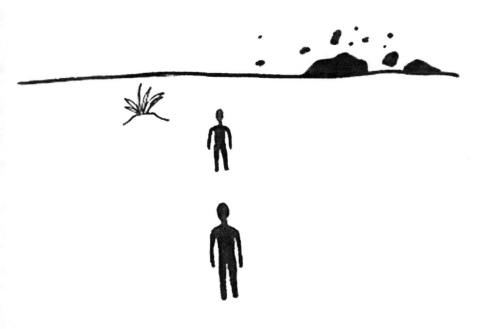

(Our mother who art
On a regular basis
Ignored
Blessed be thy tolerance
Of our continued
Hatred
Of one another's differences)

Made in the USA
San Bernardino, CA
21 June 2019